Eye, Apocalypse
Erik Fuhrer

Spuyten Duyvil
New York City

© 2021 Erik Fuhrer
ISBN 978-1-956005-30-1
Cover collage © Kimberly Androlowicz
Interior art © Erik Fuhrer

Library of Congress Cataloging-in-Publication Data

Names: Fuhrer, Erik, author.
Title: Eye, apocalypse / Erik Fuhrer.
Description: New York City : Spuyten Duyvil, [2021] |
Identifiers: LCCN 2021044574 | ISBN 9781956005301 (paperback)
Subjects: LCGFT: Poetry.
Classification: LCC PS3606.U395 E94 2021 | DDC 811/.6--dc23
LC record available at https://lccn.loc.gov/2021044574

Table of Contents

Love Affair with the Apocalypse ... 1

    Love Affair with the Apocalypse ... 3
    Rules for Encountering the Apocalypse ... 4
    Stonehenge ... 5
    Arbor Day Apocalypse ... 6
    Pocket Apocalypse ... 7
    At Home with the Apocalypse ... 8
    Meatless ... 9

Apocalyptical Time ... 11

    Apocalyptical Time ... 13
    Aurora Borealis ... 14
    Antediluvian ... 15
    The Chase ... 16
    The Apocalypse Slipped ... 17
    Big Rig Apocalypse ... 18
    Cowboy Apocalypse ... 19
    Shadowbox Apocalypse ... 20

Being the Apocalypse ... 21

    Apocalyptical Doorways ... 23
    Frank O'Hara Apocalypse ... 24
    Eye, Apocalypse ... 25
    Apocalyptical Contest ... 26
    Apocalyptical Theatre ... 27
    Being the Apocalypse ... 28
    Inner Apocalypse ... 29
    Apocalyptical Stench ... 30
    Operation Rabbithole ... 31

Odes to the Apocalypse	33
Ode to the Apocalypse 1	35
Ode to the Apocalypse 2	36
Ode to the Apocalypse 3	37
Ode to the Apocalypse 4	38
Ode to the Apocalypse 5	39
Ode to the Apocalypse 6	40
Sometimes My Body Feels Apocalyptical	41
Apocalyptical Flashes	43
Apocalyptical Silence	45
Apocalyptical Veins	46
Apocalyptical Gaze	47
Recreational Apocalypse	48
Ben Franklin Apocalypse	49
Apocalyptical Trinity	50
Apocalyptical Stare	51
Make the Apocalypse Great Again	52
Apocalyptical Hoax	53
Exhaustion	54
The Revelation of the Seven Dead	55
Notes	71
Acknowledgments	73

Love Affair with the Apocalypse

Love Affair with the Apocalypse

The apocalypse told me it loved me and swabbed me a piece of its heart
so I made us some lemonade from scratch with some lemon zest for fiber
and we drank it together on a porch swing while we exchanged vows of silence

The apocalypse told me it loved me and gave me one of its wisdom teeth
so I left it under my pillow and the next day the apocalypse brought me breakfast in bed
I ate it as it watched   wondering if the eggs were too runny

The apocalypse told me it loved me in a note that it taped to my forehead
and left the room   leaving a trail of scales in its wake that I taped to my eyelids

The apocalypse told me it loved me but never returned

The apocalypse told me it loved me   so I mourned its loss
and pasted flyers of the apocalypse all over my house

The apocalypse showed up as a guest on a late night tv show last night
it was clear it was my apocalypse and my eyelids agreed

Last night I promised myself that my apocalypse will return
once it completes the late night talk show circuit
My apocalypse is on my milk carton as a backup   I taped a flyer of it there

Rules for Encountering the Apocalypse

Don't pray to the apocalypse on your knees
Don't pen a love letter to the apocalypse
Don't open a bottle of chardonnay for the apocalypse
Don't include the apocalypse on your list of new year's resolutions
Don't whisper secrets into the apocalypse's ear
Don't make reward posters for the apocalypse when it runs away
Don't forget the apocalypse's name in the middle of the night

Stonehenge

The apocalypse goes to Stonehenge during the summer solstice
and sings Joni Mitchell's *Blue* while tripping on shrooms

The apocalypse is a teenager
The apocalypse is three billion years old
The apocalypse blows perfect smoke rings with its chipped lips

Where were you when you first met the apocalypse
What poem were you reading
Don't name a T.S. Eliot poem
Name a poem without the apocalypse in it
Hope that such a poem exists

Arbor Day Apocalypse

I first saw you in the arms of the apocalypse
You had squirrels in your hair and mice on your wrists
You were the perfect poison

The apocalypse walked in the gutters as you padded along the street
The apocalypse drank a shot of Jameson neat and chased it with a beer
as you replaced the wallet it had stolen from you with a vase of flowers
For your birthday the apocalypse bought you a vinyl copy of *Yellow Submarine*

The apocalypse left you on Arbor Day after reading your childhood copy of *The Lorax*
and you sang "all you need is love" so loud the squirrels and mice left you as well
clambering up the bark of the trees just outside your window
where you and the apocalypse used to sit on the swing set counting scars

Pocket Apocalypse

I grew a bruise that purpled
into a tiny apocalypse
which I kept in my shirt pocket
and started going to fancy cocktail parties

People would pet my apocalypse
ask if I bought it
at some boutique online store
and often abscond when I told them
that it was born of my own flesh

It's the only company I need anyway
like at night
when I put it on my pillow
feed it a clementine
and turn out the lights

At Home with the Apocalypse

Tears for Fears synthesizes on the vintage record player
as the apocalypse devours each of my records
one by one   whetting its appetite

        The apocalypse is a horn is a balloon is a putty knife
        is a cob of a corn grown in Iowa but shipped to Milwaukee
        is a stab is a hum is a *I'm going to* is a *I've already* is a

As night's pocked poppy rises in the sky
the apocalypse and I starfish
against its gruyere stare

        The apocalypse is a kitchen table
        is an egg timer pl pl plurring
        is a coffee bean roasting in my palm

Meatless

Poems with meat in them should not be written
they will only attract the apocalypse

Poems with stars in them have already been written
and now this is another one of those poems

If a poem is going to love something
it better be a villanelle

This poem loves the apocalypse
It is not a villanelle

If the apocalypse wrote a poem
it would spill its heart out
and use the word starlight

This poem prefers moonlight
but it will not argue with the apocalypse over beauty

This poem is a hymn
              a siren
a (make it strange!) tooth

Apocalyptical Time

Apocalyptical Time

A child rests inside the neck of a flower while the rest of the world hardens around it
The apocalypse licks its stone lips and swallows a sparrow and a pocket of bees
It's time to forget stories of the flood because the apocalypse has no time for Noah—
swallowed him whole a few days ago as he was waxing his kayak

This is the time in the poem where the reader falls asleep
only to feel a pinprick on their cheek
the size of the child's eye
who watches them as they fall into safety
while the world moans to move again

Inside the belly of this poem there is protection but you have to sniff out the opening

This is the time in the poem when the apocalypse sniffs out the opening
and buries itself within

This is the time in the poem when the child escapes the flower
and seals the poem up
with us all inside

This is the time in the poem when the child grows up to be the apocalypse
and we watch it through the seams in the poem as it swallows each word
one by one

Aurora Borealis

Swallow whole planets of double helixes and calculate the time it takes
to destroy an organ without quite draining all the blood from the body
Precision is key to this process so that breath is still a color we can admire
swirling in the aftermatter like the aurora borealis in a sky I will never see

If it gets to the time when the body is only a shudder
close the windows
shut the aurora borealis out
It was never here anyway
It was just an echo of light
bouncing off the body of a bluebird
who is the color of breath when it's newborn

Send the double helixes to the lab
Test for light   birdshit   an answer to the reason that the body can't stop
becoming aurora borealis

I pray to god but it is only aurora borealis
Aurora borealis is the heart when it becomes an organ rather than a pump
Aurora borealis is your face when you see an aurora borealis
Aurora borealis is double helixes spinning genetic code

Antediluvian

The apocalypse is antediluvian
its puckered tongue plicked
the bottom of Noah's ship
and was scattered about the world—
an invasive species in God's perfect land of twos—
and grew into mouths teeth bone
and every second animal
became a meal for the apocalypse
who by this point had grown large and verdant and swole

The Chase

The apocalypse listens to Janelle Monáe's *Metropolis: Suite 1 (The Chase)*
as it walks through the rainforest
Its IPod is circa 2008--vintage
like its own bones:
        circa Julius Caesar
        circa Prometheus
        circa the fire that burned way before the Gods
Zeus was real and he was swallowed by the apocalypse
Jesus was not real yet he is the one who is worshipped
instead of the apocalypse
who is backpacking around the world
and may be lying at your doorstep as you read this
Don't worry   the apocalypse is peaceful when it sleeps

The Apocalypse Slipped

The apocalypse slipped the ozone layer a cigarette without a filter
The apocalypse slipped into a sewer grate in manhattan and the earth spun three times too fast
The apocalypse slipped some methane gas between the anthropocene's wobbly teeth
The apocalypse slipped into the universe through the eye of the needle
The apocalypse slipped its body into a vintage 1920's outfit and walked the red carpet
The apocalypse slipped a secret into your ear 10 years ago when you were in traffic
The apocalypse slipped a dream into your blood the first day you dreamed in color

Big Rig Apocalypse

The apocalypse's dream of riding a big rig
through Heather, Missouri is undermined
by the fact that the only license
the apocalypse has
is a license to kill—
the apocalypse is a 1980's
Bruce Willis flick
stuck in a tower
of its own making
only it isn't Christmas
and the syringe
sticking from its arm
is not B movie grit
but a grim reality—
a herringbone stuck
in the throat
that the apocalypse coughs
to dislodge
as it fidgets
with a metal key chain
embossed
wish you were here

Cowboy Apocalypse

A John Wayne cowboy stirruped up to the apocalypse and read it its rights
The apocalypse toed a tumbleweed in the light hairnetted by shadows
and flicked a toothpick at the cowboy's shoeshined feet as it ate a fig
plucked from a tree out east where the apocalypse sat indoors at a desk
studying the habits of John Wayne cowboys and faulty movie sets

The John Wayne cowboy stuck to the script with an obligatory squint
and drew his gun on the apocalypse, aiming right for its fleshball heart pocket
The apocalypse pulled another fig out of its sack and continued to eat
as the John Wayne cowboy muttered something about a final warning

Juice spilled down the apocalypse's face as the John Wayne Cowboy began to stumble
over words: the script did not have an option built in for fig eating and John Wayne
was never recorded eating a fig or a kiwi or a full head of lettuce
all of which the apocalypse had now pulled from its sack
and set before the John Wayne cowboy who by this point was getting hungry enough
to lower his gun   grab a fig   and let the juice stain his boots with abandon

Shadowbox Apocalypse

Toothpick bones shave easily
the apocalypse learns
while building a shadowbox model of me

                The apocalypse is a red dwarf
                is Saturn's eighth ring is the big bang
                its eye the cup of our sun

                the apocalypse is not drawn to scale

Sunday nights soften the apocalypse
it takes a walk a bath goes shopping
A photo in Entertainment Weekly confirms:
the apocalypse is just like us!

Being the Apocalypse

Apocalyptical Doorways

I pass through the Apocalyptical doorway
stuffed with Tweedle Dees and carpenters
building sandcastles out of rotting meat
and twitch my bewitched nose three times in bewilderment

The apocalypse is bedazzled with walruses
whisking their whiskers through
its inner meat as I crawfish
my body past their surveillance
and stand before a giant hat beating steadily
like a watch or an army about to strike

The apocalypse is a ripple in time ripped
through the felt of my terrycloth heart
and I am in so deep that I can no longer see
light other than the flame in a rub a dub tub
of oysters simmering on low-heat

Frank O'Hara Apocalypse

I read a Frank O'Hara poem
and ate a cheese sandwich
The apocalypse replaced the sandwich
with a torch
that led me down a dark tunnel
vibrant with the rich fur coat of its odor

Its ragged breath is its own thick body
and it is this body that I follow

Suddenly the apocalypse is gone
and then it is all around me

It has swallowed me and I hang onto its tooth
until my grip slips
and its breathbody carries me
through its esophagus
and deep into its ruins

Eye, Apocalypse

I am a boneless leaf
on the dark water
of the apocalypse's eye
My mouth
its pupil
shouting in blinks

Apocalyptical Contest

The apocalypse won a contest on the radio
and dreamt of buying seven sheep
so it could bring them to a mountain in Switzerland
and live the quiet life like Daniel Day Lewis
who has become a blade of grass in the Irish countryside

The apocalypse believes in lawn maintenance
dreams one day of owning a grade-A John Deere
so he could sheer DDL clean of dust and Kerrygold

The apocalypse cherished *There Will be Blood*
and spilled oil in my body once or twice before
trying to make it to that big time end of time oil refinery
in my lungs where cows graze on my oxygen
until they develop hyperoxia and pass out into my bloodstream
moooving through my body as firmly as the apocalypse
after two straight hours on the elliptical machine
at the gym where it stares at people doing lunges in the mirror

But the apocalypse could barely afford a mower
let alone six sheep or a plane ticket
so it folded its body into a mountain
next to the New York Sports Club
in the middle of Manhattan
sleeping soundly among the traffic jams

Apocalyptical Theatre

When one door closes
another one opens and the apocalypse
slips through munching
on movie popcorn
as it consumes your life
on 8-millimeter film

In the apocalypse's theatre of doors
your body is a current
piped through electrical cords
sparking past the apocalypse's toes
and your anthem is a cat scratching
at the door of the apocalypse's heart
begging for a drop of spoiled milk

Being the Apocalypse

At Bread and Puppet
the puppets lay their bodies
in the apocalypse's footprints
forgetting the bodies
that once moved them

as John Malkovich slices
open the labyrinth
of the apocalypse
with a taut string singing
and climbs inside
a pocket of brain

When the Grateful Dead's
American Beauty plays
in the background
Malkovich dances wild
on the soft brain tissue

prompting the apocalypse
into a clumsy waltz
all the while thinking
yes
this must be beauty
as it crushes
each puppet
under its
jagged soles

INNER APOCALYPSE

The apocalypse hums into my mouth
like a downed electrical wire

The apocalypse jackets itself
behind my collarbone

The apocalypse constellates
in my throat
causing me to cough and confetti
it throughout the room
and unto a thousand tongues
held out for blessing

Apocalyptical Stench

The apocalypse
uses my face
to buy a bottle
of peaty scotch
as smoky
as its skin
which is littered
with cigarettes
still smoking

Suck it in
the apocalypse is
your father
double
spector
mouth
in enclosed spaces
a carwash with acid

Watch its skin
how it onions
as yellow-white ruins
erupt
to the surface

As the apocalypse drinks
our scotch
pours from the holes
in our body
made in Manhattan
during gridlock
and the neighbor's dog
coats its muzzle
with our doom

Operation Rabbithole

I hold onto the Mad Hatter's teeth
which jealouses the Cheshire Cat gangrene
as I rabbithole my body down the throat of the apocalypse

I've been in many apocalypse's before but this one
is like a Jan Svankmeyer film: everything is in stop motion
as if my falling is a camera shutter stuttering

The Cheshire Cat keeps flickering out of focus out of fear or just plain life
and keeps whispering that the world will end in 1972
The year Jefferson Airplane first broke up
but it is 2018
and the world still has some blood in it the Mad Hatter reminds him
his voice muffled as he spits through the teeth I am still firmly grasping
and I rabbithole the shit out of this apocalypse

Odes to the Apocalypse

Ode to the Apocalypse 1

You
a radish
overgrown
into the
thick crust
of a continent
that shifted
over me
as I wept—

I almost drowned
under your darkness

and now
you are deeply
part of me

It's like
that Ballard novel
where the characters
cannot look away
from car crashes
because I just
cannot look away
from you—
my whirlgigged heart

Ode to the Apocalypse 2

You
quarantined
but you keep
spreading--
a rhizome
rooted nowhere
squirreling through
my body—

I can feel you
in my teeth
their humming—
as if my voice
blips from your
own blinking mouth—

as if I am
Alice spilling
into the looking glass
of my own flesh

Ode to the Apocalypse 3

You
have many names
tectonic plate
earthquake
rutabaga root

Your consciousness swings from the galaxial lamppost
not a star not a sun not even the mouth of God unfolding *let there be light*

A convention of the body is that all parts will at some point sleep
You are a feast of painful silences
enfolding everywhere as subtly as an insect

You undo the impossible stroke of my body
so that I am but a sponge soaking up my own sea

I am apprehensive about the future
standing in front of you
who balled up the night and fed it to me like a pill
                                              a curse
                                              a placebo

            I swallowed

Ode to the Apocalypse 4

You
a lit match on the vaulted grass on the side of highway 80
smoldering like my eye when you are the beheld

See beauty is not a virtue when the body is a cigarette butt resting in your lips
next to your onioned tongue unraveled

You
a bee buzzing in my mouth yet I refuse to unpress my lips
because there is something about this swellsting that makes my heartbleat

You
an echo without a responder

You
the last responder when the body is doused by the river
and the only breath left calls out your name

Ode to the Apocalypse 5

You
the burning stars in my gut

You
the ripple that runs through my body
whenever I catch a glimpse of myself blinking my eyes three times to blight you

You
beautiful like eyelids are beautiful

You
the step away from the edge of the Verrazano Bridge

You
the constant reminder of that step

You
the reason I stepped away

Ode to the Apocalypse 6

You
that carnival ride that nearly ejected my 13 year old body into the yamful sky

You
the high school day after Easter when I had to tell my teachers my father died

You
the soil that I dug underneath my fingernails

You
the weight of the ceiling fan that I made sure could hold my body

You
the weight of my body

Sometimes my Body Feels Apocalyptical

I hoped it would be different when I moved halfway across the country
but it feels like the apocalypse still pulses through my brain no matter how many pills I take
as if the apocalypse isn't in me it is me
and sometimes I take a sledgehammer to my bathroom wall in the middle of the night
because I have too much energy and too little a body to contain it

People tell me just to push through it   that it will be ok
But push through what?   My own body?   How does that work?

Apocalyptical Flashes

Apocalyptical Silence

The apocalypse roots my tooth
as I speak its name
and father Abraham knocks
my jaw loose
with a wooden saw

Apocalyptical Veins

The veins of
the apocalypse: eyelids
yawning in a chair

Apocalyptical Gaze

The Apocalypse's pink stare
unfolds underfoot
as apples rot the growth

Recreational Apocalypse

Edible eyelids
beckon forth
surreptitious fish

as the Apocalypse
and I drink coffee together
underneath
the puckered meat of the sky

Ben Franklin Apocalypse

The apocalypse is the electricity
is the kite
is the eye that shed a tear
for a dying age
in which gaslight was all the rage
and darkness a blessing you had to sleep through

Apocalyptical Trinity

The apocalypse
the tongue and the swollen goat
barge into a bar

and bolt back
a bunch of blessed
Budweisers

Apocalyptical Stare

Your lidless stare—
scales of fish
against loose eyes
bobbed in applewater

Make the Apocalypse Great Again

The apocalypse is a gunshot
in a gasoline fire spitting
into the Mississippi
from a F-16 plowing
down highway 80 without
a turning signal

Apocalyptical Hoax

The apocalypse feeds
global warming a crab puff
laced with cyanide
to get rid of the competition
and declares its body
a hoax

EXHAUSTION

This poem is tired of poems about the apocalypse
The apocalypse is banished from this poem
This is not a political act
This poem is not available for a statement
This poem is tucked away safely in your pocket
Forgive the heavy smell of pecans and smoke
this poem has not bathed in a week

The Revelation of the Seven Dead

"if any one takes away from the words of the book of this prophecy, God will take away his share in the tree of life and in the holy city, which are described in this book" (Revelations 22:19)

1.

Behold every eye pierced
I am the keys of Hades

I know your apostles
have abandoned you
I know you are a two-edged witness
stumbling sacrificed practice
against the spirit's white stone
eyes like feet
strike he who searches
who keeps earthpieces

Seven dead strengthen what remains
like a blot of life

Bow down
I spew shame to anoint
those whom I love

2.

I
the first voice
clad in flashes
of voices
which are the seven creatures:

                                          lion
                                          ox
                                          man
                                          fly
                                          eagle
                                          seals

who wept to the root
of the slain
and they sang
blood from every
tongue

3.

I opened the living
creatures and I saw
bright red earth

I heard
quarts of death

I saw the witness
to be killed
behold
sunblood
and fall to fruit
shaken

4.

I sealed every shelter
They shall hunger
                thirst
                    strike scorching heat
and I will
wipe away
their eyes

5.

An angel stood
at the altar
smoke rose from the angel
filled it with fire

There were thundervoices
and an earthquake

The angel fell on the earth
and burnt up the sea

6.

I saw the bottomless
furnace smoke the seal of God
like a scorpion

Horses looked like
human faces
their scales like the bottomless
angel: his voice released plagues
the power of horses
who were worshipping demons

I
a voice
seal up the angel
who created the earth
in the days of the trumpet

Then the sky that
may have power
to turn them into blood
and the plague beast
will lie crucified

Dead bodies refuse to dwell
and fell on their faces

7.

Child red earth
devour nations fled into war

Bloodword of death

The serpent nourished
like a flood
on the sand of the sea

And I
a leopardmouth
blaspheming war tongue

I
the authority
of the first beast
dwell by the slain

I
a voice
of many waters
defiled and spotless
eternal impure passion

8.

I
harvest plagues
the beast of heaven
opened with smoke

I
a loud voice
shed the blood of god
poured the sun over him
the angel gnawed tongues in heaven
water issuing from the mouth
split into cities

I
the judgement
drunk wilderness
in a golden cup full of martyrs

9.

I
Earthbright dwelling
haunt nations
with a measure
of plagues and mourning

Alas Babylon
weep silver pearls
and human souls

The fruit
has been laid waste
and men threw
their heads out:
the blood of prophets and saints

10.

And the creatures fell crying
then opened
a white horse
clad in blood
from his mouth issues
the sun
gorged with flesh

11.

I
bottomless serpents
sealed over thousands
committed to the dead

Resurrection is prison

The earth marched
up over the saints and consumed them

Then I sat upon it
and saw the dead
opened
at the lake of fire

12.

I
a new earth
a loud voice
dwelling with men
I will wipe away
their eyes

I
polluted
murderer
the second death

I
an unclean abomination
of the Lamb
and behold
I am coming soon

Notes

Apocalyptical Contest was co-written with Abby Burns

Apocalyptical Stench was co-written with Abby Burns

The Revelation of the Seven Dead is an erasure of the Book of Revelations using the Oxford Annotated Bible. This poem is spoken from the voice of the apocalypse.

Acknowledgments

I am grateful that many of the poems from this book first appeared in the following journals:

After the Pause: Apocalyptical Doorways; At Home with the Apocalypse
Cleaver: Stonehenge
Ghost City Press: The Chase
Lotus Eater: Arbor Day Apocalypse; Exhaustion; Meatless
Maudlin House: Love Affair with the Apocalypse
Mojave Heart Review: Ode to the Apocalypse 2; Ode to the Apocalypse 3
Neologism Poetry Journal: Apocalyptical Theatre
Okay Donkey: Aurora Borealis
Punch Drunk Press: Big Rig Apocalypse
Silver Stork: Apocalyptical Stench; Apocalyptical Stare
Softblow: Apocalyptical Contest; Being the Apocalypse; Ode to the Apocalypse 6; Cowboy Apocalypse
South Broadway Ghost Society: Frank O'Hara Apocalypse
Synaeresis: Ode to the Apocalypse; Ode to the Apocalypse 4
Theta Wave: Make the Apocalypse Great Again; Apocalyptical Hoax; Ben Franklin Apocalypse
Thimble Literary Magazine: Shadowbox Apocalypse
Unlikely Stories Mark V: Apocalyptical Time; Antediluvian; Pocket Apocalypse
Zany Zygote Review: Eye, Apocalypse; Apocalyptical Silence; Apocalyptical Veins; Apocalyptical Gaze; Recreational Apocalypse

Erik Fuhrer (he/they) is the author of *in which I take myself hostage* (Spuyten Duyvil Press, 2021), *not human enough for the census* (Vegetarian Alcoholic Press, 2019), *every time you die* (Alien Buddha Press, 2019), *VOS* (Yavanika Press, 2019), and *At Root* (Alien Buddha Press, 2020). Erik holds an MFA in poetry from The University of Notre Dame and will be completing a Ph.D. in creative writing this year from the University of Glasgow.

Kimberly Androlowicz (she/her) is a visual artist who studied painting, set design, and puppetry at Bennington College. Working in acrylic and encaustic paints as well as digital art, she has provided the art for Erik Fuhrer's *not human enough for the census* (Vegetarian Alcoholic Press, 2019) and *in which I take myself hostage* (Spuyten Duyvil Press, 2021). She has had work featured online at Leopardskin and Limes and Hoot Review and has exhibited at the Heckscher Museum of Art and the B.J. spoke Gallery in Huntington, NY, and the Lubeznik Center for the Arts in Michigan City, IN.

www.ingramcontent.com/pod-product-compliance
Lightning Source LLC
Chambersburg PA
CBHW041059070526
44579CB00002B/9